Texas Temporary Tags
A Texas Peace Officer's Guide

C.R.C

Copyright © 2016 C.R.C
All rights reserved.

ISBN 13: 9781718074705

TABLE OF CONTENTS

Introduction to Temporary Tags	v
Texas's Implementation of Temporary Tags	vii
Traffic Stops on Temporary Tags	xi
Temporary Tag Quick Facts	xv
Types of Temporary Tags	**1**
72 /144-Hour Permits	3
One-Trip Permits	10
30-Day Permits	16
Texas Temporary Dealer Tags	21
Texas Temporary Buyer Tags	30
Texas Internet-Down Temporary Tags	35
Miscellaneous Temporary Permits	39
Investigation Questions and Procedures	43
Probable Cause Affidavit Examples	44
Fictitious License Plate—Class B Misdemeanor	45
Tampering with Government Record—SJF	47
Tampering with Government Record—SJF	49
Tampering with Government Record—Class A	51

INTRODUCTION TO TEMPORARY TAGS

Texas Temporary Tags were originally designed to allow dealers and motorists a window of time to acquire legitimate License Plates and Registration. However, today in Law Enforcement and in the news, it is clear that the creation of this system is facilitating an easy avenue for criminals to commit and get away with crime. This book will educate, inform and refresh your knowledge of Temporary Tags within the state of Texas. Additionally, it will allow you, as a Texas Peace Officer, to rapidly identify, process and make effective arrests regarding Altered / Fictitious Temporary License plates.

Traditionally, in most Police Departments in the State of Texas, Temporary Tags go largely unpoliced. This has led to criminals using these Temporary Tags to help cover their tracks after the commission of a crime. Take this hypothetical call, for example: a Robbery takes place at a convenience store; a witness on scene states she has the description and plate number of the vehicle. Great, right? Normally yes, but if that plate is a Temporary

Tag, there is a high likelihood that it will not come back to the vehicle or have any owner information. Not to mention that a criminal can simply swap Tags and have a completely different one on within minutes. This book is not only an advocate for enforcing of Temporary Plates and their applicable laws but also a comprehensive guide to be deployed in the field.

TEXAS'S IMPLEMENTATION OF TEMPORARY TAGS

In Texas, Counties started printing permits via their point of sale system (RTS) in 2010. In 2014, TxDMV implemented online temporary permits (webPERMITS), which allowed customers the option to purchase and print permits online—a decision that has proved instrumental to the increases in the illegal manufacture, procurement, and dissemination of Fictitious License Plates. Dealers started printing tags through the Dealer e-Tag System in 2009. All temporary permit information is updated real time and is available for query by law enforcement via TLETS and NLETS.

```
TEXAS 30 DAY PERMIT
THIS VEHICLE IS TEMPORARILY REGISTERED WITH PERMIT #

100094C

Effective Date  10-04-2017  10:00:32 AM

EXPIRES  11-03-2017  11:59:59 PM
         2016 HONDA
VIN: 1234567899TESTV1N     ISSUED BY: FLOYD CTY

RECEIPT FOR PERMIT MUST BE CARRIED IN THE VEHICLE AT ALL TIMES
```

Texas Dealer issued Temporary Tags (Buyer, Dealer, Authorized Agent) transitioned from the old style to the new style officially in December 2017. All other Temporary Tags (72 /144-Hour, One-Trip, 30-Day etc.) officially switched to the new secure style in May 2018. The new style of Temporary Tags have built-in security features that will one, make it harder for criminals to duplicate and two, easier for Law Enforcement to identify as legitimate.

A geometric lathe (2-dimensional representation of a hologram) is now displayed in the upper-right corner. When copied, the geometric lathe becomes splotchy, and areas where lines intersect become darker; areas away from intersections become lighter and look like dashed/dotted lines rather than fine lines. There is also a bar code in the lower-right corner of all new Texas Temporary Plates. When scanned the barcode on a legitimate Temporary Tag should display the following information:

Specifically, the bar code for the 144-Hour, 72-Hour, 30-Day, and One-Trip permits includes the following information in this order:

Vehicle model year, Vehicle make, VIN, Permit #, Effective date and time, Expiration date and time, Place of issuance, Permit type.

* The bar code for the One-Trip permit also includes Origin, Intermediate, and Destination points as the last item.

That being said, there could still be the old-style dealer temporary permits on the road for up to a year past the official implementation date. This is because Dealers can print Buyer Tags in advance for issuance when the Internet is unavailable, and they are unable to print a Buyer Tag. These tags are referred to as Buyer Internet-Down Tags. Additionally, the Dealer Vehicle and Agent Specific Tags can be printed in advance and the expiration date set by the dealer, so there is a chance you will still see those.

TRAFFIC STOPS ON TEMPORARY TAGS

In addition to all of your regular traffic stops, listed below are a few Temporary Tag related Pretext stops to add to your repertoire.

TRANSPORTATION CODE; Sec. 502.095. ONE TRIP OR 30 DAY PERMITS.

- 30-Day / One-Trip Permits must be displayed in the rear window of a vehicle, not the license plate holder of a vehicle; if you see this, then you have a violation under this chapter.

TRANSPORTATION CODE; Sec. 503.0626. DEALER'S AND CONVERTER'S TEMPORARY TAG DATABASE.

- When running a vehicle's Temporary Dealer / Converter plate through TCIC / NCIC, it is required by law that the return show detailed information about the Dealer / Converter. This includes Dealership name and address. If the return does not come back with this information, you have a legal stop under this chapter. *Important note: Vehicle information is not required for most Dealer Temporary Tags.

TEXAS ADMINISTRATIVE CODE; Sec. 215.151 Temporary Tags, General use Requirements and Prohibitions

- A dealer <u>SHALL</u> secure a temporary tag to a vehicle in the license plate display area located at the rear of the vehicle, so that the entire temporary tag <u>IS VISIBLE</u> and <u>LEGIBLE AT ALL TIMES, INCLUDING WHEN THE VEHICLE IS BEING OPERATED.</u>
- <u>All printed information</u> on a temporary tag must be visible and <u>may not be covered or obstructed by any plate holder or other device or material.</u>

- If a 30 Day Permit is not securely affixed to its designated area and is flying up and down in the wind, you have a violation under this chapter.

TRANSPORTATION CODE; Sec. 503.0631. BUYER'S TEMPORARY TAG DATABASE.

- When running a vehicle's Temporary Buyers Tag through TCIC / NCIC, it is required by law that the return show detailed information about the Buyer. If the return does not come back with this information, you have a legal stop under this chapter.

TRANSPORTATION CODE; Sec. 503.068. LIMITATION ON USE OF DEALER'S LICENSE PLATES AND TAGS.

- Dealer Temporary Tags have specific uses, such as in transit from Austin house to dealership, or for customers to conduct a Test Drive. Dealer Temporary Tags are not to be used for personal use under this chapter; if you develop Reasonable Suspicion to believe the vehicle is being used for personal use, then you have a legitimate Traffic Stop under this section and a citable offense.

TEMPORARY TAG QUICK FACTS

- All legitimate Temporary Tags should have only **1** alphanumeric character in its sequence (ie. 12**F**3456), anymore and the Tag is not legitimate.
- A vehicle can only ever be issued one Buyer Tag per owner / VIN for the life of the ownership by that person. If the subject's vehicle is showing to have an expired Buyers Tag in TCIC/ NCIC but the physical plate date is currently effective, then the plate is not legitimate.
- A Texas Temporary Tag will be issued on official TxDMV letterhead, equipped with watermarks.
- A return of "NO RECORD RTS" database, indicates that the paper tag does not exist in the Texas Department of Motor Vehicle Registration and Title System.

TYPES OF TEMPORARY TAGS

72 /144-HOUR PERMITS

FACTS AND OFFICAL USES:

The TxDMV issues 72 / 144-Hour permits for the movement of laden trucks, truck-tractors, semitrailers, or motorbuses on State highways. A 72 /144-Hour permit can only be legally issued to commercial vehicles and buses owned by residents of the USA, Mexico and Canada. A motorist operating a CMV with a 72 / 144-Hour permit must still show proof liability insurance that meets Texas minimum requirements.

72 / 144-Hour permits may only be purchased and acquired from two legitimate sources: a Local County Tax Assessor-Collector office, or a TxDMV Regional Service Center. **(Key to remember when building probable cause to show that the Tag is Fictitious and or criminally acquired.)**

Common Violations:

TRANSPORTATION CODE; Sec. 503.067. UNAUTHORIZED REPRODUCTION, PURCHASE, USE, OR SALE OF TEMPORARY TAGS.

- Look into how they acquired the Temporary Tag and who made the Temporary Tag for them; if not from any of the above listed sources, you have an offense. The fact they are operating a vehicle with an Unauthorized (Fictitious) Temporary Tag is an offense under this section.

- **TRANSPORTATION CODE; Sec. 503.094. CRIMINAL PENALTY.** Holds the criminal levels for this section, ranging from Class C Misdemeanor to a State Jail Felony.

TRANSPORTATION CODE; Sec. 504.944. OPERATION OF VEHICLE WITH WRONG LICENSE PLATE.

- Occasionally the Temporary Plate will be valid and legitimate but belong to another vehicle. This is a citable offense that can lead to an impounded vehicle and inventory after seizing the plate.

TRFANSPORTATION CODE; Sec. 504.945. WRONG, FICTITIOUS, ALTERED, OR OBSCURED LICENSE PLATE.

- This offense should be enforced under **subsection a)** 4, Class B Misdemeanor. Any alteration, addition, subtraction to the information displayed on the Temporary Tag, makes the Tag Fictitious; as it is no longer what a legitimate Tag would display. This is enforced through custody arrest and seizing of the plate and impounding of the vehicle. There is no culpable mental state, as this does not fall under Penal Code. Stated simply, if the Tag is displayed on the vehicle, and it is Fictitious, then there is an offense.

PENAL CODE; Sec. 37.10. TAMPERING WITH GOVERNMENTAL RECORD.

- *Martinez v. State* has already held that Temporary Tags are considered Government records under subsection: b) anything required by law to be kept by others for information of government.
- With this charge you need to articulate that the suspect either admitted to knowing the Plate was Fictitious, manufactured /

made the Fictitious Plate, or show through a preponderance of the evidence that a reasonable person would have known it was false.
- Proving a suspect knew the Plate was false can be accomplished in numerous ways:
    - Where did the suspect acquire the Plate? Was it form a legitimate source as per TxDMV?
    - How long has the suspect had the vehicle? The longest period for a plate to be valid is 60 days.
    - Plate specifics: Have they been issued more than one Buyer Tag? Are there multiple letters in Temporary Plate? etc.

6 C.R.C

TxDMV Certified Examples of 72 / 144-Hour Permits
*Use these certified examples as a tool to point out inconsistences with suspected Fictitious Plates.

OLD FORMAT

TEXAS 72-HOUR PERMIT
THIS VEHICLE IS TEMPORARILY REGISTERED WITH PERMIT #

100092C

Effective Date 10-04-2017 09:53:14 AM

EXPIRES 10-07-2017 09:53:14 AM

2015 MACK

VIN: TESTV1N1234567899   ISSUED BY: FLOYD CTY

RECEIPT FOR PERMIT MUST BE CARRIED IN THE VEHICLE AT ALL TIMES
VALID IN TEXAS ONLY

TEXAS 144-HOUR PERMIT
THIS VEHICLE IS TEMPORARILY REGISTERED WITH PERMIT #

100095C

Effective Date 10-04-2017 10:02:33 AM

EXPIRES 10-10-2017 10:02:33 AM

2015 MACK

VIN: TESTV1N1234568799   ISSUED BY: FLOYD CTY

RECEIPT FOR PERMIT MUST BE CARRIED IN THE VEHICLE AT ALL TIMES
VALID IN TEXAS ONLY

8 C.R.C

NEW FORMAT

TEXAS 72-HOUR PERMIT
THE VEHICLE TEMPORARILY REGISTERED WITH PERMIT #

102924F

2018 RAM

Expires **MAY 18, 2018**

VIN: 3C6TRVCG6JE108114
Issued By: COLLIN CTY
VALID IN TEXAS ONLY

ONE-TRIP PERMITS

FACTS AND OFFICAL USES:

The TxDMV issues One-Trip Permits for the temporary movement of unladed vehicles. A One-Trip Permit is only valid for a period of 15 days.

A One-Trip Permit is valid for one trip only between the point of origin and the point of destination and the intermediate point as shown on the receipt. A motorist operating a vehicle with a One-Trip Permit must still show proof liability insurance that meets Texas minimum requirements.

One-Trip Permits may only be purchased and acquired from two legitimate sources: A Local County Tax Assessor-Collector office or a TxDMV Regional Service Center. **(Key to remember when building probable cause to show that the Tag is Fictitious and / or criminally acquired.)**

Permit Display

A One-Trip Permit must be displayed in the rear window of the vehicle. If the vehicle does not have a rear window, the operator must carry the permit and receipt in the vehicle any time the vehicle is in transit.

Common Violations:

TRANSPORTATION CODE; Sec. 503.067. UNAUTHORIZED REPRODUCTION, PURCHASE, USE, OR SALE OF TEMPORARY TAGS.

- Look into how they acquired the Temporary Tag and who made the Temporary Tag for them; if not from any of the above listed sources, you have an offense. The fact they are operating a vehicle with an Unauthorized (Fictitious) Temporary Tag is an offense under this section.
- **TRANSPORTATION CODE; Sec. 503.094. CRIMINAL PENALTY.** Holds the criminal levels for this section, ranging from Class C Misdemeanor to a State Jail Felony.

TRANSPORTATION CODE; Sec. 504.944. OPERATION OF VEHICLE WITH WRONG LICENSE PLATE.

- Occasionally the Temporary Plate will be valid and legitimate but belong to another vehicle. This is a citable offense that can lead to an impounded vehicle and inventory after seizing the plate.

TRFANSPORTATION CODE; Sec. 504.945. WRONG, FICTITIOUS, ALTERED, OR OBSCURED LICENSE PLATE.

- This offense should be enforced under **subsection a)** 4, Class B Misdemeanor. Any alteration, addition, subtraction to the information displayed on the Temporary Tag, makes the Tag Fictitious; as it is no longer what a legitimate Tag would display. This is enforced through custody arrest and seizing of the plate and impounding of the vehicle. There is no culpable mental state, as this does not fall under Penal Code. Stated simply, if the Tag is displayed on the vehicle, and it is Fictitious, then there is an offense.

PENAL CODE; Sec. 37.10. TAMPERING WITH GOVERNMENTAL RECORD.

- *Martinez v. State* has already held that Temporary Tags are considered Government records under subsection: b) anything required by law to be kept by others for information of government.
- With this charge you need to articulate that the suspect either admitted to knowing the Plate was Fictitious, manufactured / made the Fictitious Plate, or show through a preponderance of the evidence that a reasonable person would have known it was false.
- Proving a suspect knew the Plate was false can be accomplished in numerous ways:
    - Where did the suspect acquire the Plate? Was it form a legitimate source as per TxDMV?
    - How long has the suspect had the vehicle? The longest period for a plate to be valid is 60 days.
    - Plate specifics: Have they been issued more than one Buyer Tag? Are there multiple letters in Temporary Plate? etc.

TxDMV Certified Examples of One-Trip Permits

*Use these certified examples as a tool to point out inconsistencies with suspected Fictitious Plates.

OLD FORMAT

```
TEXAS ONE-TRIP MC PERMIT
THIS VEHICLE IS TEMPORARILY REGISTERED WITH PERMIT #

100093C

Effective Date 10-04-2017 09:56:55 AM
EXPIRES 10-19-2017 11:59:59 PM
2014 HARLEY DAVIDSON
VIN: TESTV1N1234567899        ISSUED BY: FLOYD CTY
        ORIGINATION POINT: AUSTIN, TEXAS
        DESTINATION POINT: OKLAHOMA CITY, OKLAHOMA
RECEIPT FOR PERMIT MUST BE CARRIED IN THE VEHICLE AT ALL TIMES
```

14 C.R.C

NEW FORMAT

TEXAS ONE-TRIP MC PERMIT
THE VEHICLE TEMPORARILY REGISTERED WITH PERMIT #

102920F

2016 YAMA

Expires **MAY 30, 2018**

VIN: JYARM06E7GA008384
Issued By: COLLIN CTY

TEXAS ONE-TRIP PERMIT
THE VEHICLE TEMPORARILY REGISTERED WITH PERMIT #

102922F

1995 CHEV

Expires **MAY 30, 2018**

VIN: 2GCEC19Z5S1246117
Issued By: COLLIN CTY

30-DAY PERMITS

FACTS AND OFFICAL USES:

The TxDMV issues 30-Day Permits for the temporary movement of a vehicle that is still subject to Texas Registration laws. 30-Day Permits are valid for a period of 30 days from the effective date listed on the permit. A motorist operating a vehicle with a 30-Day Permit must still show proof liability insurance that meets Texas minimum requirements. <u>No more than three 30-Day permits will be legally issued per vehicle.</u>

30-Day Permits may only be purchased and acquired from two legitimate sources: A Local County Tax Assessor-Collector office or a TxDMV Regional Service Center. **(Key to remember when building probable cause to show that the Tag is Fictitious and or criminally acquired.)**

Permit Display

A 30-Day Permit must be displayed in the rear window of the vehicle. If the vehicle does not have a rear window, the operator must carry the permit and receipt in the vehicle any time the vehicle is in transit.

Eligible Use

30-Day Permits are available for passenger vehicles, motorcycles, private buses, trailers, and semitrailers with a gross weight not exceeding 10,000 lbs., and for light commercial vehicles not exceeding a gross vehicle weight of 10,000 lbs. A commercial vehicle exceeding a gross weight of 10,000 lbs. is eligible for the permit if operating unladen.

Common Violations:

TRANSPORTATION CODE; Sec. 503.067. UNAUTHORIZED REPRODUCTION, PURCHASE, USE, OR SALE OF TEMPORARY TAGS.

- Look into how they acquired the Temporary Tag; who made the Temporary Tag for them? If not from any of the above listed sources, you have an offense. The fact they are operating a vehicle with an Unauthorized (Fictitious) Temporary Tag is an offense under this section.
- **TRANSPORTATION CODE; Sec. 503.094. CRIMINAL PENALTY.** Holds the criminal levels for this section, ranging from Class C Misdemeanor to a State Jail Felony.

TRANSPORTATION CODE; Sec. 504.944. OPERATION OF VEHICLE WITH WRONG LICENSE PLATE.

- Occasionally the Temporary Plate will be valid and legitimate but belong to another vehicle. This is a citable offense that can lead to an impounded vehicle and inventory after seizing the plate.

TRFANSPORTATION CODE; Sec. 504.945. WRONG, FICTITIOUS, ALTERED, OR OBSCURED LICENSE PLATE.

- This offense should be enforced under **subsection a)** 4, Class B Misdemeanor. Any alteration, addition, subtraction to the information displayed on the Temporary Tag, makes the Tag Fictitious, as it is no longer what a legitimate Tag would display. This is enforced through custody arrest and seizing of the plate and impounding of the vehicle. There is no culpable mental state, as this does not fall under Penal Code. Stated simply, if the Tag is displayed on the vehicle, and it is Fictitious, then there is an offense.

PENAL CODE; Sec. 37.10. TAMPERING WITH GOVERNMENTAL RECORD.

- *Martinez v. State* has already held that Temporary Tags are considered Government records under subsection: b) anything required by law to be kept by others for information of government.
- With this charge you need to articulate that the suspect either admitted to knowing the Plate was Fictitious, manufactured / made the Fictitious Plate, or show through a preponderance of the evidence that a reasonable person would have known it was false.
- Proving a suspect knew the Plate was false can be accomplished in numerous ways:
  - Where did the suspect acquire the Plate? Was it form a legitimate source as per TxDMV?
  - How long has the suspect had the vehicle? The longest period for a plate to be valid is 60 days.
  - Plate specifics: Have they been issued more than one Buyer Tag? Are there multiple letters in Temporary Plate? etc.

TxDMV Certified Examples of 30-Day Permits
*Use these certified examples as a tool to point out inconsistences with suspected Fictitious Plates.

OLD FORMAT

TEXAS 30 DAY PERMIT
THIS VEHICLE IS TEMPORARILY REGISTERED WITH PERMIT #

100094C

Effective Date 10-04-2017 10:00:32 AM

EXPIRES 11-03-2017 11:59:59 PM

2016 HONDA

VIN: 1234567899TESTV1N   ISSUED BY: FLOYD CTY

RECEIPT FOR PERMIT MUST BE CARRIED IN THE VEHICLE AT ALL TIMES

20 C.R.C

NEW FORMAT

TEXAS 30 DAY PERMIT
THE VEHICLE TEMPORARILY REGISTERED WITH PERMIT #

102921F

2010 FORD

Expires **JUN 14, 2018**

VIN: 1FTFW1EV3AFB34049
Issued By: COLLIN CTY

TEXAS TEMPORARY DEALER TAGS

FACTS AND OFFICAL USES:

The TxDMV allows Dealers who hold a General Distinguishing Number license to issue Dealer temporary tags, buyer's temporary tags, and Internet-down temporary tags for each type of vehicle the dealer is licensed to sell. This Temporary Tags when ran must either have either vehicle information or agent information (dealership info). A Dealer Temp Tag is only valid for a period of 1–60 days. More than one tag may be issued to any agent, but only one tag may be assigned to any specific vehicle at a time.

Eligible Use

Temporary Dealer Tags can only be used for vehicle demonstration, transit from dealer to dealer, Auction, reconditioning, or on a loaner car given by the dealership while a customer's car is being worked on. Cannot be used by dealership personnel for personal use.

Example of Temporary Dealer Authorized Agent Tag Return

SELECTION REQUEST: TEMPORARY TAG   67K4973

TEMPORARY TAG: 67K4973   VALID:2017/09/28 00:00:00--2017/11/27 00:00:00
YR: 0 MAK:

DEALER TEMPORARY TAG – AGENT

NAME: Montgomery T Moore, 495 35TH ST NE, PARIS, TX, 75460

Common Violations:

TRANSPORTATION CODE; Sec. 503.068. LIMITATION ON USE OF DEALER'S LICENSE PLATES AND TAGS.

- Dealer Temporary Tags have specific uses, such as in transit from Austin house to dealership, or for customers to conduct a Test Drive. Dealer Temporary Tags are not to be used for personal use under this chapter. If you develop Reasonable Suspicion to believe the vehicle is being used for personal use, then you have a legitimate Traffic Stop under this section and a citable offense.

TRANSPORTATION CODE; Sec. 503.067. UNAUTHORIZED REPRODUCTION, PURCHASE, USE, OR SALE OF TEMPORARY TAGS.

- Look into how they acquired the Temporary Tag; who made the Temporary Tag for them? If not from any of the above listed sources, you have an offense. The fact they are operating a vehicle with an Unauthorized (Fictitious) Temporary Tag is an offense under this section.

- **TRANSPORTATION CODE; Sec. 503.094. CRIMINAL PENALTY.** Holds the criminal levels for this section, ranging from Class C Misdemeanor to a State Jail Felony.

TRANSPORTATION CODE; Sec. 504.944. OPERATION OF VEHICLE WITH WRONG LICENSE PLATE.

- Occasionally the Temporary Plate will be valid and legitimate but belong to another vehicle. This is a citable offense that can lead to an impounded vehicle and inventory after seizing the plate.

TRFANSPORTATION CODE; Sec. 504.945. WRONG, FICTITIOUS, ALTERED, OR OBSCURED LICENSE PLATE.

- This offense should be enforced under **subsection a)** 4, Class B Misdemeanor. Any alteration, addition, subtraction to the information displayed on the Temporary Tag, makes the Tag Fictitious, as it is no longer what a legitimate Tag would display. This is enforced through custody arrest and seizing of the plate and impounding of the vehicle. There is no culpable mental state, as this does not fall under Penal Code. Stated simply, if the Tag is displayed on the vehicle, and it is Fictitious, then there is an offense.

PENAL CODE; Sec. 37.10. TAMPERING WITH GOVERNMENTAL RECORD.

- *Martinez v. State* has already held that Temporary Tags are considered Government records under subsection: b) anything required by law to be kept by others for information of government.
- With this charge you need to articulate that the suspect either admitted to knowing the Plate was Fictitious, manufactured / made the Fictitious Plate, or show through a preponderance of the evidence that a reasonable person would have known it was false.

- Proving a suspect knew the Plate was false can be accomplished in numerous ways:
    - Where did the suspect acquire the Plate? Was it form a legitimate source as per TxDMV?
    - How long has the suspect had the vehicle? The longest period for a plate to be valid is 60 days.
    - Plate specifics: Have they been issued more than one Buyer Tag? Are there multiple letters in Temporary Plate? etc.

TEXAS TEMPORARY TAGS 25

TxDMV Certified Examples of Temporary Dealer Permits

*Use these certified examples as a tool to point out inconsistences with suspected Fictitious Plates.

OLD FORMAT

```
TEXAS DEALER
VEHICLE OWNED BY PULLER USED CARS #2
THE VEHICLE TEMPORARILY REGISTERED WITH STATE UNDER TAG #
96M9795
EXPIRES 11-28-2017
Authorized Agent Tag
```

26 C.R.C

TEXAS CONVERTER

THE VEHICLE TEMPORARILY REGISTERED WITH STATE UNDER TAG #

43B0391

EXPIRES **11-13-2017**

2014 FORD
VIN 1FMCU0GX5EUD02922

NEW FORMAT

TEXAS DEALER
THE VEHICLE TEMPORARILY REGISTERED WITH TxDMV UNDER TAG #

01A0367

2015 FORD

Expires **DEC 03, 2017**

VIN: 1FA6P8TH9F5342216

Owned by: DODGE COUNTRY LTD

28 C.R.C

TEXAS DEALER
THE VEHICLE TEMPORARILY REGISTERED WITH TxDMV UNDER TAG #

01A0366

Authorized Agent Tag

Expires **DEC 03, 2017**

Owned by: DODGE COUNTRY LTD

TEXAS TEMPORARY TAGS

TEXAS CONVERTER
THE VEHICLE TEMPORARILY REGISTERED WITH TxDMV UNDER TAG #

01A0368

2015 FORD

Expires **FEB 01, 2018**

VIN: 1FA6P8TH9F5342217

Converter: TEREX UTILITIES, INC

TEXAS TEMPORARY BUYER TAGS

FACTS AND OFFICAL USES:

In the State of Texas, a Temporary Buyer Tag is only issued with a retail sale. The vehicle and buyer's information must be entered in to the E-Tag system and be available to Law Enforcement upon running the vehicle. Buyer Temporary Tags must be displayed in the rear license plate holder, and the owner must have the Buyer receipt in the vehicle always. The absence of this receipt can help articulate falsity and probable cause for crimi-nal activity regarding the plate. A Buyer Tag is only good for a period of 60 days. Additionally, only one Buyer Tag can be issued per person / vehicle.

Common Violations:

TRANSPORTATION CODE; Sec. 503.067. UNAUTHORIZED REPRODUCTION, PURCHASE, USE, OR SALE OF TEMPO-RARY TAGS.

- Look into how they acquired the Temporary Tag; who made the Temporary Tag for them? If not from any of the above listed sources, you have an offense. The fact they are operating a vehicle

with an Unauthorized (Fictitious) Temporary Tag is an offense under this section.
- **TRANSPORTATION CODE; Sec. 503.094. CRIMINAL PENALTY.** Holds the criminal levels for this section, ranging from Class C Misdemeanor to a State Jail Felony.

TRANSPORTATION CODE; Sec. 504.944. OPERATION OF VEHICLE WITH WRONG LICENSE PLATE.

- Occasionally the Temporary Plate will be valid and legitimate but belong to another vehicle. This is a citable offense that can lead to an impounded vehicle and inventory after seizing the plate.

TRFANSPORTATION CODE; Sec. 504.945. WRONG, FICTITIOUS, ALTERED, OR OBSCURED LICENSE PLATE.

- This offense should be enforced under **subsection a)** 4, Class B Misdemeanor. Any alteration, addition, subtraction to the information displayed on the Temporary Tag, makes the Tag Fictitious, as it is no longer what a legitimate Tag would display. This is enforced through custody arrest and seizing of the plate and impounding of the vehicle. There is no culpable mental state, as this does not fall under Penal Code. Stated simply, if the Tag is displayed on the vehicle, and it is Fictitious, then there is an offense.

PENAL CODE; Sec. 37.10. TAMPERING WITH GOVERNMENTAL RECORD.

- *Martinez v. State* has already held that Temporary Tags are considered Government records under subsection: b) anything required by law to be kept by others for information of government.
- With this charge you need to articulate that the suspect either admitted to knowing the Plate was Fictitious, manufactured /

made the Fictitious Plate, or show through a preponderance of the evidence that a reasonable person would have known it was false.
- Proving a suspect knew the Plate was false can be accomplished in numerous ways:
    - Where did the suspect acquire the Plate? Was it form a legitimate source as per TxDMV?
    - How long has the suspect had the vehicle? The longest period for a plate to be valid is 60 days.
    - Plate specifics: Have they been issued more than one Buyer Tag? Are there multiple letters in Temporary Plate? etc.

TEXAS TEMPORARY TAGS 33

TxDMV Certified Examples of Temporary Buyer Permits

*Use these certified examples as a tool to point out inconsistences with suspected Fictitious Plates.

OLD FORMAT

```
TEXAS BUYER
THE VEHICLE TEMPORARILY REGISTERED WITH STATE UNDER TAG #

06W8981

EXPIRES 11-28-2017
2014 FORD
VIN 1FMCU0GX5EUD02970
SELLER: 1500 BARTON SPRINGS INC
```

34 C.R.C

NEW FORMAT

TEXAS BUYER

THE VEHICLE TEMPORARILY REGISTERED WITH TxDMV UNDER TAG #

01A0365

2015 FORD

Expires **DEC 03, 2017**

VIN: 1FA6P8TH9F5342215

Seller: DODGE COUNTRY LTD

TEXAS INTERNET-DOWN TEMPORARY TAGS

FACTS AND OFFICAL USES:

In the State of Texas, a Dealer must use an Internet-Down Tag if at the time of sale, the Dealer cannot connect to the E-Tag system. Tags and receipts are preprinted by dealer with the assigned number. Buyer and vehicle info are hand printed by the dealer. The Internet-Down tag is valid for a period of 60 days and must be displayed in the rear license plate holder.

When dealing with these Tags, look for errors and or alterations to already written numbers.

Common Violations:

TRANSPORTATION CODE; Sec. 503.067. UNAUTHORIZED REPRODUCTION, PURCHASE, USE, OR SALE OF TEMPORARY TAGS.

- Look into how they acquired the Temporary Tag; who made the Temporary Tag for them? If not from any of the above listed

sources, you have an offense. The fact they are operating a vehicle with an Unauthorized (Fictitious) Temporary Tag is an offense under this section.
- **TRANSPORTATION CODE; Sec. 503.094. CRIMINAL PENALTY.** Holds the criminal levels for this section, ranging from Class C Misdemeanor to a State Jail Felony.

TRANSPORTATION CODE; Sec. 504.944. OPERATION OF VEHICLE WITH WRONG LICENSE PLATE.

- Occasionally the Temporary Plate will be valid and legitimate but belong to another vehicle. This is a citable offense that can lead to an impounded vehicle and inventory after seizing the plate.

TRFANSPORTATION CODE; Sec. 504.945. WRONG, FICTITIOUS, ALTERED, OR OBSCURED LICENSE PLATE.

- This offense should be enforced under **subsection a)** 4, Class B Misdemeanor. Any alteration, addition, subtraction to the information displayed on the Temporary Tag, makes the Tag Fictitious, as it is no longer what a legitimate Tag would display. This is enforced through custody arrest and seizing of the plate and impounding of the vehicle. There is no culpable mental state, as this does not fall under Penal Code. Stated simply, if the Tag is displayed on the vehicle, and it is Fictitious, then there is an offense.

PENAL CODE; Sec. 37.10. TAMPERING WITH GOVERNMENTAL RECORD.

- *Martinez v. State* has already held that Temporary Tags are considered Government records under subsection: b) anything required by law to be kept by others for information of government.
- With this charge you need to articulate that the suspect either admitted to knowing the Plate was Fictitious, manufactured / made the

Fictitious Plate, or show through a preponderance of the evidence that a reasonable person would have known it was false.
- Proving a suspect knew the Plate was false can be accomplished in numerous ways:
  - Where did the suspect acquire the Plate? Was it form a legitimate source as per TxDMV?
  - How long has the suspect had the vehicle? The longest period for a plate to be valid is 60 days.
  - Plate specifics: Have they been issued more than one Buyer Tag? Are there multiple letters in Temporary Plate? etc.

TxDMV Certified Examples of Temporary Buyer Permits

*Use these certified examples as a tool to point out inconsistences with suspected Fictitious Plates.

NEW FORMAT

TEXAS BUYER - INTERNET DOWN
THE VEHICLE TEMPORARILY REGISTERED WITH TxDMV UNDER TAG #

01A0342

Expires
Year: Make:
VIN:
Seller: DODGE COUNTRY LTD

MISCELLANEOUS TEMPORARY PERMITS

This section will briefly cover and depict a few rarely used Temporary Tags, to give familiarity with them in case you are ever presented with one.

Transmit Permit

If a subject buys a car or truck and the seller keeps the Texas license plates, the Transit Permit will allow them to legally drive the vehicle home or to their local county tax office.

Only one Transit Permit may be issued per vehicle. Only passenger vehicles and light trucks are eligible.

The Transit Permit is valid for 5 days (maximum) from date of issuance; the start date is the day the permit is printed.

40 C . R . C

TxDMV Certified Examples of Miscellaneous Temporary Permits

*Use these certified examples as a tool to point out inconsistences with suspected Fictitious Plates.

TEXAS TEMPORARY INSIGNIA
VALID FOR 60 CALENDAR DAYS ONLY. ANY ALTERATION VOIDS THIS INSIGNIA.

B58BB

2010 CHEV

Expires **JUL 14, 2018**

VIN: 3GCXKTE27AG297543
Issued By: COLLIN CTY

TEXAS TEMPORARY INSIGNIA
VALID FOR 60 CALENDAR DAYS ONLY. ANY ALTERATION VOIDS THIS INSIGNIA.

EARKL

2018 FORD

Expires **JUL 14, 2018**

VIN: 1FTEW1E53JKC81607
Issued By: COLLIN CTY
THIS PERSONALIZED MESSAGE IS PENDING APPROVAL BY THE TxDMV.

42 C.R.C

TEXAS FACTORY DELIVERY PERMIT
THE VEHICLE TEMPORARILY REGISTERED WITH PERMIT #

102923F
2018 CHEV
Expires **JUN 14, 2018**

VIN: 1GCGSCEN7J1188043
Issued By: COLLIN CTY

INVESTIGATION QUESTIONS AND PROCEDURES

- Affect a Traffic Stop.
- Make the scene safe.
- Interview the driver of the vehicle beside the altered / fictitious tag.
- Check to see if the check engine light is on. If so, document for evidence.
- If it is a Dealer Tag, ask if they are a Dealer.
- Ask how much they paid for the vehicle.
- Ask who sold them the vehicle.
- Ask if they have the title.
- Ask if they know the address of the person who sold them the vehicle.
- Ask who put the Tag on the vehicle.
- Ask where they got the tag.
- Take pictures of the Title, Tag, and any other documentation of evidentiary purposes.
- Seize the fictitious / altered Tag.

PROBABLE CAUSE AFFIDAVIT EXAMPLES

This chapter has a few examples of Probable Cause affidavits that have been accepted by Judges and successfully issued bonds for the arrestees. All private, and identifying information has been redacted.

FICTITIOUS LICENSE PLATE - CLASS B MISDEMEANOR

On 06/18/2018 at approximately 18:10, while working as a two officer unit, Officer ▇▇▇ along with Officer ▇▇▇ were traveling Northbound on Webberville Rd, when they observed the following vehicle: TXLP Temp (Texas Buyer): 01C0385, BLK, 2004, INFIN expiring **07/12/2018**, traveling northbound on Webberville Rd. Officer ▇▇▇ ran the vehicle through TCIC/ NCIC and received the following return via MDT (Mobile Data Terminal); the vehicle's Temporary tag came back with the following return: **NO RECORD IN RTS DATABASE**. The vehicle was ran twice before initiating a traffic stop for Reasonable Suspicion of a Fictitious Plate.

Officer ▇▇▇ made contact with the driver of the vehicle, identified as ▇▇▇ and questioned her over the origins of the Temp Tag. ▇▇▇ stated she had just purchased the car off of Craigslist about a month ago. ▇▇▇ stated the vehicle was hers.

During further investigation of the Temporary Plate, Officer ▇▇▇ discovered the following additional discrepancies: The first was that the Temporary Plate was issued in the old style of Tag, which the TxDMV no longer uses. Even when comparing the Temp Tag to the TxDMV old style Tags the following discrepancies were noted: The font for all of the information was incorrect, The letter sizing on the TEXAS BUYER was incorrect, The VIN and Seller information were located in the wrong area of the Plate, and the Temp Tag had the verbiage **"RECEIPT FOR PERMIT MUST BE CARRIED IN THE VEHICLE AT ALL TIMES"** where there should be no verbiage on a legitimate Texas Buyer Temp Tag. For these reasons, and those listed previous, Officer ▇▇▇ deemed the Tag Fictitious and placed ▇▇▇ under arrest for Fictitious License Plate.

TAMPERING WITH GOVERNMENT RECORD – SJF

On 06/21/2018 at approximately 15:15 while working as a two Officer unit, Officer ███████ and Officer ███████ observed a white vehicle traveling Westbound on Oak Springs Blvd. Officer ███ observed what appeared to be a Fictitious Plate on the rear of the vehicle. Before Officers could turn around and conduct a stop on the vehicle, they observed another ███ unit tailing the vehicle. Officer ███ and Officer ███████ responded to a traffic Stop conducted by Officer ███ on the vehicle they had observed. The vehicle was identified as:

-- 1995 White, Oldsmobile 4D, Tx Temp Tag: 349764F VIN: ███████

Officer ███ had pulled the vehicle over for Expired Temporary Plates. Officers then approached the vehicle and made contact with the following occupants:

-- ███████ ***arrestee/front passenger***
-- ███████ ***driver/involved***
-- ███████ ***arrestee/rear passenger***

Officer ▌ made contact with ▌ and asked for insurance. ▌ also stated the vehicle was his and that he had recently purchased it from someone on Face Book. ▌ stated he just left the TXDOT because he was trying to get a valid license plate. Officer ▌ then asked ▌ why he was stopped. ▌ stated because his license plate was expired. Officer ▌ then asked ▌ if the license plate was fake, ▌ stated it was fake, and his friend changed the numbers on the license plate. Officer ▌ observed the following discrepancies on Texas temp Tag: 349764F:

- -- Expires 06-17-2018 (the numbers 6,17 are fictitious and glued over the original expiration numbers
- -- the actual TCIC/NCIC return: 349764F VALID:2018/04/16 09:30:36--2018/05/16 23:59:59

▌ was then placed under arrest for Tampering with a Government Record. While in custody ▌ would make the following Res Gestae statements in regards to the Temporary Tag: ▌ admitted to Officer ▌ and Officer ▌ numerous times that he was aware the temp tag on the white Oldsmobile at the time of the traffic stop was in fact fake, and that he observed his friend change the numbers, which made the plate appear valid so that he could drive the vehicle around until he got actual legitimate Plates for the vehicle. Officers on scene had confession that ▌ knew the Tags were in fact false and that he was attempting to pass his vehicle off as a lawfully registered vehicle as to avoid being stopped by Police.

TAMPERING WITH GOVERNMENT RECORD – SJF

On 06/11/2018 at approximately 17:40 hrs, while working as a two officer unit, Officer ▇▇▇ along with Officer ▇▇▇ were traveling Westbound on Loyola Ln, when they observed the following vehicle: TXLP Temp (Texas 30 Day Permit): 86HK66H, WHI, FORD, expiring **05/04/2018** traveling Westbound on Loyola Ln. Officer ▇▇▇ first alerted to the vehicle because the Temp Tag displayed three alphanumeric characters, when legitimate Temporary Tags only display one alphanumeric character. Officer ▇▇▇ ran the vehicle through TCIC/ NCIC and received the following return via MDT (Mobile Data Terminal); the vehicle's Temporary tag came back as **NO RECORD IN RTS DATABASE**. Due to the aforementioned discrepancies between the physical Plate and the TCIC / NCIC return, Officer ▇▇▇ pulled the vehicle over for Reasonable Suspicion of Fictitious Plate.

Officers pulled the vehicle over and made contact with the arrestee and driver, ▇▇▇. Officer ▇▇▇ began to question ▇▇▇ about the plate. ▇▇▇ stated the following: ▇▇▇ had the vehicle for approximately 6 months, by his own account. ▇▇▇ stated he was issued Temporary plates when he purchased the vehicle. Officer ▇ asked ▇ what he did when the old Temporary Tag expired, ▇ Stated that he went to "some dude at a house" to purchase and print him the current Temporary Tags on his vehicle. Based on ▇ statements Officer ▇ had further reason to believe that ▇ took party to the unauthorized reproduction and use of a fictitious Temporary Tag. This is because there are only three legitimate places to obtain a Texas 30-day permit, and they are as follows: Austin Regional Service Center, Online, or Tax-Assessor Collection Office.

During further investigation of the Temporary Plate, Officer ▇ discovered the following additional discrepancies: The Temp 30-Day Permit, the Temporary Tag, listed both the Make and Model of the vehicle, whereas a legitimate Tag would only list the Make. Additionally, the ink, font and spacing of the lettering were all off. For these reasons, and those listed previous, Officer ▇ deemed the Tag Fictitious / false and had Probable Cause to believe that ▇ not only knew the Temporary Tag was fake but that he requested that it be made so that he could continue to drive his unregistered vehicle on public streets. It is held that Temporary Tags are anything required by law to be kept by others for information of government, therefore making them Government Records.

TAMPERING WITH GOVERNMENT RECORD – CLASS A

On 07/15/2018 at approximately 18:00 while working as a single Officer unit, Officer ▇▇▇ observed a white vehicle traveling Southbound on Webberville Blvd. Officer ▇▇▇ observed what appeared to be a Fictitious Plate on the rear of the vehicle. Officer ▇▇▇ ran the vehicle through TCIC / NCIC and received the following information: the Temporary Tag came back as a **30 Day Permit, Valid: 05/30/2018 – 06/29/2018, 2007 DODGE 4D.** Based on the return Officer ▇▇▇ pulled the vehicle over for improperly displayed Temporary Tag, a violation of TC. 502.095. 30-Day permits are required to be displayed in the rear window of a vehicle.

Upon pulling the vehicle over, Officer ▇▇▇ observed the Temporary Tag to have a listed expiration date of **08/03/2018,** which was different from the TCIC / NCIC expiration date of **06/29/2018.** Additionally, the Temporary Tag was that of the old style TxDMV permits, which are no longer legal on Texas roadways, but also had elements of the new secure tags such as a barcode at the bottom of the Tag. The Permit did not match any legal plate issued by the TxDMV. Based on the affiants training and experience with Texas paper tags, altered/ fictitious are used to mask offenses such as stolen vehicles, salvage vehicles, unregistered motor vehicles or motor vehicles that cannot pass State mandated emissions safety inspections.

Officer ▇▇ then made contact with the driver of the vehicle identified as the arrestee ▇▇▇▇▇▇▇▇▇▇▇▇▇▇▇▇▇▇▇▇▇ and the passenger identified as ▇▇▇▇▇▇▇▇▇▇▇▇▇▇▇▇▇. Officer ▇▇ interviewed ▇▇▇▇ in regards to the vehicle. ▇▇▇▇ stated the following: ▇▇▇▇ claimed he only had the car for 7-8 days, as a loaner from a friend. The friend was later identified as ▇▇▇▇▇▇▇▇▇▇▇▇▇▇▇▇▇▇. ▇▇▇▇ stated he planned on giving the car back around Monday. Officer ▇▇ then asked ▇▇▇▇ for ▇▇▇▇'s number, which ▇▇▇▇ gave freely.

Officer ▇▇ later called ▇▇▇▇ on scene, and learned the following information: ▇▇▇▇ stated that he had sold ▇▇▇▇ the vehicle approximately 3 months ago. The vehicle used to belong to his daughter, but she got in a wreck and was unable to complete all the repairs. ▇▇▇▇ stated that ▇▇▇▇ took over repairing the vehicle and making it operational again. Officer ▇▇ asked if when ▇▇▇▇ bought the vehicle did it had paper plates on it. ▇▇▇▇ stated yes, but that they had recently expired because the vehicle could not pass inspection. ▇▇▇▇ stated that he and his daughter had already gotten two 30 day permits for the vehicle in the past and knew they were coming up on their limit. ▇▇▇▇ stated ▇▇▇▇ knew of all the repairs that were required on the vehicle, and that the vehicle could not pass State inspection to be registered legally. Most importantly ▇▇▇▇ stated clearly that when he sold the vehicle to ▇▇▇▇, he and his daughter had recently went to the TxDMV off of ▇▇▇▇ to get a 30-Day permit, so ▇▇▇▇ could have time to fix the car. ▇▇▇▇ stated that the plates on the vehicle should have been expired, and that the plates he put on the vehicle originally were from the DMV, which Officer ▇▇ observed not to be the case, as the plate in ▇▇▇▇ possession was deemed fictitious. Additionally, ▇▇▇▇ could not furnish a registration receipt for his displayed 30-Day permit, which by Texas Transportation

Code should always be in the vehicle. The Permit was also displayed in a regular zip lock bag.

It is the affiant's belief that ███████████████ intentionally and knowingly presented and used the altered / fictitious 30-Day Permit, a government record, with knowledge of its falsity and with intent that it be taken as a genuine governmental record in violation of Texas Penal Code.

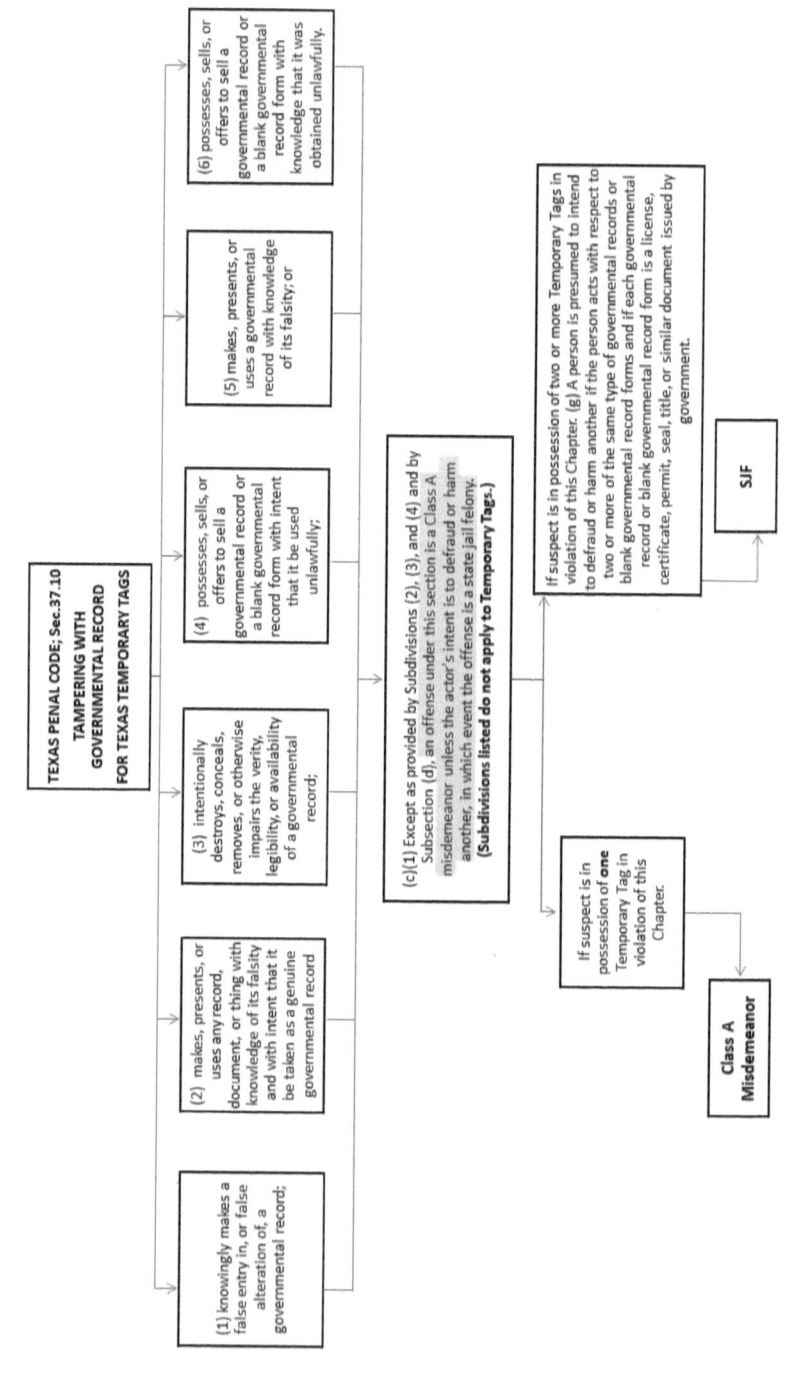

This is a professional development resource, and all examples listed throughout this book are Official depictions from the TxDMV Vehicle Titles and Registration Division, or actual in the field depictions from Law Enforcement Officers. If a Tag you come across does not match up with its corresponding example shown throughout this book, exactly as shown, then the Tag is Altered/ Fictitious.

SPECIAL THANKS TO:

The Texas Department of Motor Vehicles
    Vehicle Titles and Registration Division

Author's Notes:

Please leave a review on Amazon, if you found this book helpful, and refer a shift mate.

www.ingramcontent.com/pod-product-compliance
Lightning Source LLC
Chambersburg PA
CBHW031543210526
45464CB00003B/1119